THE *Kennedy* COLLECTION

A NATION WORTH FIGHTING FOR

THE *Kennedy* COLLECTION

A NATION WORTH FIGHTING FOR

D. JAMES KENNEDY, Ph.D.
Edited by Karen VanTil Gushta, Ph.D.

D. James Kennedy
MINISTRIES™
TRUTH IN *Action*®

Fort Lauderdale, FL

THE KENNEDY COLLECTION
A NATION WORTH FIGHTING FOR

By D. James Kennedy, Ph.D.
Edited by Karen VanTil Gushta, Ph.D.

© 2015 D. James Kennedy Ministries

All rights reserved. Written permission must be secured from the publisher to use or reproduce any part of this book, except for brief quotations in critical reviews or articles.

Scriptures are taken from the King James Version of the Bible and the New King James Version, copyright ©1982 by Thomas Nelson, Inc. Used by permission. All rights reserved.

ISBN: 978-1-929626-44-1

Jacket and Interior Design: Roark Creative, www.roarkcreative.com

Published by:
    D. James Kennedy Ministries
    P.O. Box 7009
    Albert Lea, MN 56007
    1-800-988-7884
    www.DJamesKennedyMinistries.org
    letters@truthinaction.org

Printed in the United States of America

CONTENTS

Introduction — 9

Building a Christian Nation — 11

Lest We Forget — 29

The Cost of Freedom — 45

A Nation Worth Fighting For — 65

About the Author — 79

*Blessed is the nation
whose God is the Lord…*

— Psalm 33:12a

INTRODUCTION

∽

Have Americans lost the will to fight for our nation and our freedoms?

In the title chapter, Dr. Kennedy poses the question, "Is this nation worth fighting for? Is it worth my dying for?" The lives of thousands of Americans have now been sacrificed on foreign soil in response to unprovoked aggression in an effort to end "this awful scourge of terrorism," as Dr. Kennedy put it. But as Christianity's influence wanes, we are facing enemies without and within, and the question is: Will America turn back to God or will it turn away from the One who has blessed America beyond measure and protected it from its enemies?

In chapter one, "Building a Christian Nation," Dr. Kennedy traces the foundations that first made America "a city set on a hill." Our Pilgrim forefathers came with the express purpose of establishing a colony "for the glory of God, and the advancement of the Christian faith." That vision also guided the Founders and as John Quincy Adams noted, this nation connected for the first time "the principles of civil government with the precepts of Christianity."

America is quickly forgetting that heritage. Therefore,

in chapter two, "Lest We Forget," Dr. Kennedy challenges us to remember not only the purposes of our Founders, but also the One whose invisible hand of providence first prepared and protected this land from other colonizers. Had any of them succeeded, America would not have become a haven of religious freedom, nor would the Gospel of Jesus Christ and His grace have gained such a strong foothold.

In chapter three, "The Cost of Freedom," Dr. Kennedy observes that the burning flame of liberty, which so moved our Founders, "is burning very weakly in America today." Our religious liberty is in jeopardy. Our only hope is that a great revival will sweep across this land and turn hearts to seek God, the Great Emancipator; for those who have truly been liberated in Christ will also seek freedom in the political realm.

May the Lord use these sermons to kindle the flame of liberty in the heart of every reader. Only He can bring change to this nation in the midst of the present turmoil. As Dr. Kennedy says in the conclusion of the final chapter, "A Nation Worth Fighting For," God wants each of us in His army, "the army of Christ, the army of life—that forever army that is changing and will change the whole world…. You are all welcome, and no one is 4F."

Karen Van Til Gushta, Ph.D.
D. James Kennedy Ministries
Fort Lauderdale, Florida

Chapter 1

BUILDING A CHRISTIAN NATION

*If the foundations are destroyed,
What can the righteous do?*

— Psalm 11:3

A NATION WORTH FIGHTING FOR

Today I would like to consider not only the *building* of a Christian nation, but also the *rebuilding* of the same. For there is no doubt in the mind of anyone who has studied the history of our nation's founding that our forefathers built a Christian nation. In the last fifty years, there are those who have worked assiduously to tear it down, to destroy the foundations. Now, however, there is a renewed interest and desire on the part of many millions in this country to see it rebuilt again.

Nevertheless, there are many who do not even know that this ever was a Christian nation. I was interviewed recently by Alan Colmes—a liberal talk show host—about one of our new books, *What If America Were a Christian Nation Again?* During the entire interview, he focused on one single word. Can you imagine which one it was? It was the word "again."

"How," said Colmes, "could America become a Christian nation again, when America *never was* a Christian nation?"

Colmes is a pretty intelligent fellow, and I am sure he speaks for millions of people who, when you say America was founded as a Christian nation, would look at you as if you had just arrived from Mars (or in case you are a woman—from Venus), and you obviously know nothing about the wonderful secular nation we have inherited.

Another time, when I was on *The Merv Griffin Show* and I was debating with Sam Donaldson, his comment on the subject was, "Well, there may have been a *few* Christians around when America was founded, but one thing is certain, they gave us a secular nation."

A LOOK AT HISTORY

Well, Sam, let's take a look at history. "A few Christians around"? In 1776, at America's founding, historians tell us that 98.4 percent of the people in America professed themselves to be Protestant Christians, 1.4 percent professed to be Roman Catholic Christians, and the remaining .2 of 1 percent professed themselves to be Jewish. That means that 99.8 percent of the American people in 1776 professed themselves to be Christians.[1]

Yes, Sam, there were a few Christians around.

They gave us a secular nation? Let's look at that statement also. The word "secular" comes from the Latin *saecularis*, which means a view of civil society or education devoid of the religious element. Is that what they gave us? Let us run the camera back and see what the tape looks like when this country began.

- George Washington had just taken the oath of office, to which he appended his own words—

---

[1] Benjamin Hart, "The Wall That Protestantism Built: The Religious Reasons for the Separation of Church and State," *Policy Review*, Fall 1988, p. 44.

which have been repeated ever since, "So help me, God."

- He then bent over and kissed the Bible on which he had just taken his oath.

- He then led the entire Congress, House and Senate, two blocks down the street for a two-to-three-hour-long service of worship in his own Anglican Church.

- And Washington presided over the Congress as they chose chaplains for the military, a chaplain for the Senate, and a chaplain for the House of Representatives.

All of that was at taxpayer's expense! A civil society without reference to the religious element? Hardly!

Secularism has been described as a view of life with no thought of God or of a future life. It is like a "smoked dome" placed over the city of man—no one can see up to God and no one can see forward beyond the black pit of the grave. That is secularism. It is an utterly hopeless view of life. Secularists are without God and without hope in the world. Thank God that is not what the Founders of this country believed!

Building a Christian Nation

In 1776 there was not anywhere on this planet a secular nation. Prior to 1776, throughout the history of the whole planet, there had never been such an institution as a "secular nation." It did not exist. The first one was established in France just a few years after the American Revolution.

Our revolution was based upon God. The French Revolution was based upon humanistic atheism, and it ended with blood running in the streets. Tens of thousands of people were guillotined and the revolution was a gigantic disaster. France became a secular nation. To demonstrate this, a woman was set up on the altar in Notre Dame Cathedral and worshiped as the Goddess of Reason. They even tried to get rid of the Sabbath day and establish a ten-day week, but that didn't work and they had to abandon the whole concept. France had dissolved into chaos.

No. There never had been, and there was not at the time of the American Revolution anywhere in the world a secular nation. The Founders of our country could not have imagined anything even close to that. In fact, when they discovered what was happening in France a few years later, they were appalled. It was abhorrent to them.

No, Sam, you need to read up on your history before commenting on how this country was started.

WHY THEY CAME TO AMERICA

We could go back to the very beginning. We could go back to the Pilgrims. We could go back before that to Christopher Columbus. We could go back even farther—we could go back 1,000 years ago to Leif Ericson. Many people don't know much about him. He was born in Iceland. His father was Eric the Red—a very flamboyant gentleman who lived in Norway until he murdered a man; then he fled for his life to Iceland, where Leif was born.

When Leif achieved manhood, he wanted to return to his ancestral home. So he took a trip to Norway, and there he ran into Christians, and he was converted to Christ. After staying there for a little while and learning more about the faith, what he wanted most of all was to take the Gospel back to Iceland and beyond. So he got some missionaries to go with him. They went to Iceland, preached the Gospel for some time, and then they moved on to Greenland. They continued to preach the Gospel and then they moved on to the northeast tip of North America—most likely in what is now Newfoundland, Canada. Here is the first contact this continent had with Europeans—and they most likely came to preach the Gospel.

If we go ahead to the 1600s, more than 500 years later, we find that the Pilgrims set sail from England and landed at Plymouth. Why did they come? What was their purpose in coming to these shores?

One of America's presidents in the early part of the 20th century, was asked, "What is the business of America?" I think that is a provocative question: "What is the business of America?"

Here is his completely secular answer: "The business of America is business."

Now, I certainly would not want to say that business is not of great importance, because it is. God commands us to work to earn our living, to provide for our families, others, and ourselves as we can, but that is not "the business of America." America was founded by people who loved God, trusted in the divine grace of Jesus Christ, and desired most of all to make Him known to others.

We don't have to rely on someone's opinion about this. We can hear it directly from them. William Bradford was the historian and governor of Plymouth Plantation. He wrote the only history of the time. He is the only source. He was governor for decades. He said that before the Pilgrims even left England, they wrote these words about their reason for coming. Was it for gold? Let's see what Bradford said:

> …a great hope and inward zeal they had of laying some good foundation (or at least to make some way thereunto) for the propagating and advancing of the Gospel of the Kingdom of Christ in those

remote parts of the world: Yea, but though they should be but even as stepping-stones unto others for the performing of so great a work.

And so they have been. More missionaries have gone forth from America than any other country in the world and more money has been raised for missions. One of the ministries of this church has now taken the Gospel to every nation on earth. Their great desire has been fulfilled.

HOW AMERICA BEGAN

The Pilgrims came because of an inward zeal and a great hope of propagating and advancing the Gospel to the far ends of the earth. When the Pilgrims actually arrived here, before they set foot on land, they met in the captain's cabin of the Mayflower and wrote what has been called the "birth certificate of America"—the Mayflower Compact. How does the Mayflower Compact begin? "Seeing that we need to set up some kind of a secular organization here to run this thing, we will...."

No! That is not what they said. They began with the words, "In the name of God. Amen." That is how America began. The Pilgrims explained exactly why they had come to these shores:

... having undertaken for the glory of God, and

advancement of the Christian faith ... a voyage to plant the first colony in the northern parts of Virginia....

Having undertaken "for the glory of God and the advancement of the Christian faith." That is why they came, and that is what they did. They advanced the Christian faith and continued to do so for generations.

If we go forward in time to the end of the nineteenth century, the Supreme Court of the United States looked at the question of *whether this was or was not* a Christian nation and carefully deliberated the question. Finally they reached a unanimous decision, the *Trinity* decision, which they issued in 1892; exactly 400 years after Columbus made his great voyage. They said: "These references add a volume of unofficial declarations to the mass of organic utterances that this is a religious people ... a Christian nation." This was the opinion of the Supreme Court of the United States, the highest court in this land.

Let us look at John Quincy Adams, who was probably one of the most, if not the most, brilliant presidents we ever had. He was the sixth president of the United States and the son of John Adams. When he went to France as just a young man, he was not really a believer in the deity of Christ. He was a Unitarian. But he wrote back home and said that he had, through his reading, become convinced of the deity of Christ. Someone wrote back to him and said, "How could you possibly believe something like that? What Bible have you been reading? Must be some kind of cultist thing."

He wrote back and said (I'm paraphrasing), "Well, I read two different English versions of the Bible; then I read the Greek and the Hebrew Bibles, two different versions of the Latin Bible, as well as three in French and two in German, and several others. Any other questions?"

This *is* what Adams said: "The highest glory of the American Revolution was this…." (I would like to have a group of college students finish that sentence.) What was it that the American Revolution accomplished? Some might say it got rid of the Stamp Act, it dissolved our relationship with England, and it made us free and independent. However, that is *not* what President John Quincy Adams said. What he said was, "The highest glory of the American Revolution was this: it connected in one indissoluble bond the principles of civil government with the precepts of Christianity."

That doesn't sound like "separation of church and state" to me! But there have been atheists and humanists and agnostics and other "tics" of that sort who, with their dissolving solutions have tried their best to separate the principles of civil government from the precepts of Christianity. That is not what our Founders gave us.

Not at all!

THE FIRST AMENDMENT

After the Constitution was written and the ten amendments were added, probably the most influential and massive commentary on the Constitution written by any justice of the Supreme Court was produced by Joseph Story. Story was appointed to the Supreme Court by James Madison, who is often called "the architect of the Constitution." He had enough confidence in Joseph Story to appoint him to the Supreme Court.

In Story's three-volume *Commentaries on the Constitution of the United States*, first published in 1833, he wrote about the First Amendment—"Congress shall make no law respecting an establishment of religion or prohibiting the free exercise thereof." Story says:

> The real object of the amendment was, not to countenance, much less to advance Mahometanism, or Judaism, or infidelity, by prostrating Christianity; but to exclude all rivalry among Christian sects [denominations], and to prevent any national ecclesiastical establishment, which should give to an hierarchy the exclusive patronage of the national government. It thus cut off the means of religious persecution, (the vice and pest of former ages,) and of the subversion of the rights of conscience in matters of religion, which

had been trampled upon almost from the days of the Apostles to the present age.

Some may say, "Well, the First Amendment tells us that there should be a 'separation of church and state.'" I am sure you have heard that there should be a "wall of separation" between church and state.

That is fairly close: It's just that the First Amendment never mentions a *wall*. It never mentions a *separation*; it never mentions a *church*; and it never mentions a *state*! Other than that, that statement is pretty close. Yet most Americans have been told by the ACLU and their friends that the First Amendment says there should be a "wall of separation between church and state." Folks, it is just not so.

You may say, "That is just your opinion, but you are just a preacher. What do you know?" Let me give you an opinion of someone more knowledgeable than I about these things. He said this:

> There is simply no historical foundation for the proposition that the framers intended to build the "wall of separation" [between church and state] ... the "wall of separation between church and State" is a metaphor based on bad history, a metaphor which has proved useless as a guide to judging. It should be frankly and explicitly abandoned.

The gentleman who said that, William Rehnquist, is the current Chief Justice of the Supreme Court of the United States.

Shall I repeat what he said? "The 'wall of separation between church and state' is a metaphor built on bad history, a metaphor which has proved useless as a guide to judging. It should be frankly and explicitly abandoned." This metaphor is an utter distortion of the First Amendment and not a condensation of it, says Chief Justice William Rehnquist.

TWIN PILLARS OF HAPPINESS

Religion is not the threat to government the liberal mind thinks it is. In fact, George Washington, the father of our country, said, "True religion offers the government its surest support." It does not undermine it. Washington also said that religion and morality are the twin pillars of human happiness in this world, and the man who labors to undermine those pillars does not deserve the title of "patriot."

Yet how many atheists today are working diligently to undermine the pillars of religion and morality? They would get rid of God, get rid of the commandments of God, get rid of any of His moral rules—and still claim to be patriots. However, such a person, said George Washington, does not deserve the title.

Daniel Webster was probably the most eloquent man this country ever produced. In a discourse he delivered at Plymouth, Massachusetts, in 1820, commemorating the 200th anniversary of the Pilgrims' settlement of New England, he concluded:

> Finally, let us not forget the religious character of our origin. Our fathers were brought hither by their high veneration for the Christian religion. They journeyed by its light and labored in its hope. They sought to incorporate its principles with the elements of their society and to diffuse this influence through all their institutions—civil, political, or literary.
>
> Let us cherish these sentiments and extend their influence still more widely; in full conviction that that is the happiest society which partakes in the highest degree of the mild and peaceful spirit of Christianity.

Indeed, "Let us not forget the religious character of our origin." This is a Christian nation. These and hundreds of other references would point that out. I have read the constitutions of all fifty of our states. I have read the inaugural addresses of all of our presidents. All of them, without exception, reference God. This is not a secular, godless, atheistic state, as our young people are being taught in school—nothing like that—in spite of the continued efforts to turn it into just that. Our Founders built a godly nation, which we have inherited, and in the lifetime of virtually everyone here, we have seen it torn down brick by brick. But it can be rebuilt. It was built by men. It is being torn down by men. It can be rebuilt by men as well.

IT IS ALL ABOUT GOD

Thankfully, in the last several decades there has been a revival of interest in the founding of this country and in what it was intended to be, and what it can be again. More and more Christians are rising up, whereas before, the majority of Christians in this country didn't even vote. If we would just get all the Christians out to vote, these problems would disappear with alacrity.

One person put it this way: What we need to do is not only vote, but we need to vote correctly. Basically, there is only one subject and one name on the ballot and in the voting booth with you. Always, in every consideration, there is God. If we would learn to vote with that awareness—"What would God want me to do? How would He want me to vote?"—it would make all the difference. This nation would quickly be restored to godliness if God were seen to be, as we believe Him to be, everywhere—in our homes, our schools, our work, and our play. We need to see Him in the voting booth.

When I was getting ready to vote the other morning, I started talking to a lady in line behind me. We had a nice discussion about a number of things. We got close to the door, and she leaned over very close to me and said, "May I ask you a very personal question?" (We are now three people from the door, after an hour and twenty minutes.)

I said, "Sure, what?"

She said, "Who are you going to vote for?"

I looked around to see if there was a camera somewhere. I didn't know if I was being set up or something. Not seeing one, I said, "I'll be happy to answer your question. You understand that I did not force this upon you. You asked me. Is that correct?"

She said, "Yes." (I wanted that on the tape, if there was one.)

I told her whom I was going to vote for—then I told her why. I pointed out that it is all about God. It is not about how much money you are going to get in Social Security, or how big a raise you are going to get, or how much of this or that you are going to get. When you read all of the writings of the Founding Fathers, you will notice there is never a mention of anything that any of them is going to get. They were all laying their lives, their fortunes, and their sacred honor on the line—and we are thinking selfishly, "What am I going to get?"

When you think about how you are going to vote, God is there with you. Ask yourself, "What would God want me to do?"

I told her, "You need to consider the moral issues that are involved, not only in the presidency, but mostly through the courts and those who are appointed. What is that going to produce?"

One decision by the Supreme Court has resulted to date in the cruel deaths of over 45 million American babies. How do you think God would have wanted you to vote on that issue? It is all about God. That is what politics ultimately is. That is what our Founders believed it was about: "In the name of God." "For the glory of God." "For the advancement of His kingdom." That is why they came. That is not why most Americans vote, and that is not how they vote. But if you want to see this nation transformed, you must begin to see God in the voting booth with you.

God alone will change this nation. May we recognize that He is the sovereign Lord of this world and of the universe. This is our Father's world. We rejoice in that fact. And yet we have grieved Him by ten thousand faults, turning away from Him and turning to the folly and the foolishness of men who have corrupted our families, who have corrupted our schools, who have corrupted our courts, who have corrupted our government, who have corrupted our media, and who have corrupted our amusements. How this has wounded Him!

So may we ask His help in remembering that it is all about Him and that if we advance His cause—His Kingdom—He will provide all things that are necessary for us.

⤺

This is an edited version of the sermon "Building a Christian Nation," which Dr. D. James Kennedy delivered to his congregation at Coral Ridge Presbyterian Church on October 31, 2004.

Chapter 2

LEST WE FORGET

Oh, give thanks to the Lord, for He is good!
For His mercy endures forever.
Let the redeemed of the Lord say so,
Whom He has redeemed from the hand of the enemy,

— Psalm 107:1-2

A NATION WORTH FIGHTING FOR

This is Memorial Day weekend and today we remember. We remember those who died for the freedoms we enjoy. At least we should. The Bible is filled with admonitions to remember. There are a dozen or more words translated "remember."

Remember.... Remember. We should, indeed, remember with gratitude those who laid down their lives in the many wars that have been fought to gain our freedoms—especially, most precious of all to us—the freedom of religion.

Did you know that America is unique because this was the first nation in the history of this planet to have freedom of religion? Some of you think it is just a commonplace sort of thing. But until America's founding, religious tyranny prevailed all over the globe. Gradually some nations rose to the level of religious tolerance, like England, but only in America was full religious freedom granted for the very first time.

The Bible tells us, *"Known to God from eternity* [the creation of the earth] *are all His works"* (Acts 15:18). This continent, hidden between two great oceans, was reserved by God for that religious freedom—for that expression of the true Gospel of Jesus Christ—a land where His Word would be read, where He would be worshiped, where He would be trusted, and His Gospel would be proclaimed both here and throughout the whole world.

THE PROVIDENCE OF GOD

Therefore, I would like us to remember not only those men and women who laid down their lives in the wars our nation fought, but also the One who fought the longest to give us what we enjoy most—the One who is often the most forgotten.

There is a strange lament we find in Scripture: *"My people have forgotten Me days without number"* (Jeremiah 2:32). How can that be? Today I would like to remember Him who "plants His footsteps in the sea and rides upon the storm"—the invisible hand of that One whose providence in centuries gone by brought the Pilgrims to Plymouth Rock and established this nation of religious freedom, which we have, alas, almost lost in our generation! I want us to remember the providence of God, the unseen, the invisible hand of Him who was the real Architect and General of our freedom.

In 1778, George Washington wrote a letter to a friend in which he said:

> …The hand of Providence has been so conspicuous in all of this that he must be worse than an infidel that lacks faith, and more wicked that has not gratitude to acknowledge his obligations [of gratitude to God].

There are millions of such people in this country today who will not acknowledge the gratitude owed to the invisible hand of Him who "rides upon the storm." The Bible says that God is the God of storms. And so, on this Memorial Day weekend, may we consider the invisible hand of Him who "plants His footsteps in the sea and rides upon the storm," and who brought us to this land of freedom.

I have consulted many of the historical works of the greatest of Colonial historians—Bancroft, Creasy, Campbell, Smith, Williams and a dozen others. I have learned things you are not likely, in some cases, to have learned in school about the formation of this uniquely Christian nation from which the Gospel has gone forth to the ends of the world as from no other nation in history—a nation where the Bible has been loved and respected.

In the hymn "God Moves in a Mysterious Way," we are told that "He plants His footsteps in the sea and rides upon the storm." This *God of Storms* is the One who created this nation. He certainly demonstrated that He is the Lord of the Sea when He opened the Red Sea before the children of Israel as they were fleeing the tyrannical armies of the Pharaoh. Then He closed those waves upon the army of Egypt and the riders and horses were cast into the sea.

Let us then consider how God has, for our sake, shown Himself as the invisible God—the Lord of the Sea, the Hand of Providence.

THE PERSIAN THREAT

It was "D Day"—well, not really "D" day for Europe. It was "P" Day and it was the Persians who were knocking at the door of Greece as the vast empire of Persia under Darius had decided to invade Europe. This massive army landed on the beaches of Marathon in Greece. The Greek army was pitifully tiny by comparison. There was no contest. Surely Europe was about to become Zoroastrian, and you today—since this country was founded by European settlers—would be worshiping Ahura Mazda, the god of the Persians.

However, that is not what God intended for this country. The *God of Stormy Rains* caused the rains to fall not only on the plains of Spain, but upon the plains of Marathon, which had a huge marsh that was now filled with water. The vast army of Persia was up to its knees in water, so the smaller more mobile groups of Greeks around their sides picked the great Persian army to pieces.

The word went out and a messenger, Pheidippides, ran twenty-two miles to tell the Athenians that the Persians had been defeated. The Persians were not easily put off, however, so ten years later Darius' son Xerxes sent his vast fleet of more than 1,200 ships to attack Greece. The navy of Greece was little prepared to deal with them, but that *One who plants His footsteps in the sea and rides upon the storm* caused the winds to blow and the waves to rise up and six hundred Persian warships sank to the bottom of the Mediterranean. The Greeks finished off the rest and the Persian threat was withdrawn.

THE MUSLIM ATTEMPTS

If we were not to be Zoroastrians, we could have become Muslims. Over the top of this church, which would instead be a Mosque, there would then be the crescent moon of Islam. Since Europe was the birthplace of this nation, consider again what God did.

In 711 A.D., the Moors, the vast North African horde of Arabs and Berbers who were fanatically committed to Islam, crossed over at Gibraltar, entered the Iberian Peninsula, and conquered all of Spain. Then the relentless lust for conquest eventually drove their seemingly invincible armies over the Pyrenees Mountains into central Europe. They entered France and destroyed Toulouse and Bordeaux and one city after another, consolidating their advances and gathering a vast booty of gold and silver along the way. They moved two-thirds of the way across France until they came to the city of Tours, where they were met by Charles Martel, "Charles the Hammer," and his army of Christian Franks.

It seemed that the soldiers of the crescent were so laden down with the booty they had gathered, they were not fit to fight, so their general told them to lay it all down.

Then the armies faced each other. For seven days they stared each other down across the vast plain. Finally the Islamic general commanded them to charge. And so they came—this wall of Arab horsemen galloping across the plain. Martel and his infantry in heavy armor stood firm against the onslaught.

Then God sent a whisper. It was simply this: "The enemy is stealing our spoils." First one column of horsemen reeled and turned to go back and defend their goods, and then another and another and another. Then the rest of the vast army, not knowing why the others were turning around, decided that a retreat had been called and suddenly the whole army reeled around and began to flee!

Martel and his forces attacked the fleeing Muslim cavalry. Their leader was killed, and when the day was over there had been tremendous defeat. The Muslim effort to subjugate all of Europe came to an end, and seven years later, Martel drove them out of France altogether.

But the Muslims weren't finished with this land. Several centuries before Columbus sailed, they sent a whole fleet to cross the Atlantic. They were intrepid sailors who were going to cross the Atlantic to find what was on the other side of the ocean and to found and colonize the new land, which could have been America. *But He who plants His footsteps in the sea and rides upon the storm* blew upon the waters, the waves rose up to Heaven and came down, and the entire fleet sank to the bottom of the

Atlantic Ocean and was never heard from again.

THE SPANISH EXPLORATION

We were not destined to be either Zoroastrians or Muslims, but we could have been a number of other things. For example, it would not have been hard for us to be Spanish. Most of Latin America, Mexico, Central America, and South America did become Spanish and we could have been too. Columbus was headed right for the Carolinas. Things were getting very bad on the ship. The sailors were terrified, thinking they were going to sail off the end of the world. They were ready to panic, mutiny, throw the admiral overboard and sail back to Europe, when someone sighted "Land ho!" Off to the southwest they spotted land, so the ships turned away from the Carolinas and headed south. As they got closer, several days later, they discovered that what they had seen was not land, but storm clouds on the horizon.

So they turned their ships northwest. They were heading for what is now Jacksonville, Florida. Then God sent a flight of seagulls. They crossed the bow of the ship. No doubt they were heading to land, thought the sailors, and that was southwest. The command was, "Follow those birds," and they missed America altogether.

We could have had a Spanish form of religion that at that time repressed the Bible, distorted the Gospel, and defended religious tyranny with the Inquisition. But God said "Nay." So it was not to be.

THE FRENCH ATTEMPTS

We could have been French. Fourteen years before the Pilgrims landed at Plymouth Rock, the French sent three groups of ships to colonize this continent. The first two were blown back by strong winds, but the last group made it closer, and they were dashed upon the shoals of Cape Cod. That attempt was withdrawn. Yet some years later, after the British had occupied this land and established New England, the French were determined to change it to "New France." The Duke d'Anville was given 64 ships and 11,000 men with orders to "consign Boston to flames, ravage New England and waste the British West Indies."

Before he could reach New England, however, d'Anville's fleet was continuously beset by storms and gales along the way and his soldiers and sailors were ravaged with disease. Shortly after they arrived in Nova Scotia, d'Anville died and his replacement, the Marquis de la Jonquière, inherited the order to ravage Boston.

But the governor of Massachusetts proclaimed a day of fasting to pray for deliverance from "the present peril." In Boston's Old South Church, the Reverend Thomas Prince stood before his congregation and prayed, "Deliver us from our enemy! Send Thy tempest,

Lord, upon the waters to the eastward! Raise Thy right hand. Scatter the ships of our tormentors and drive them hence. Sink their proud frigates beneath the power of Thy winds!"

As he was praying, there suddenly was heard a sound. So startling was the sound that he stopped praying. The shutters on the church began to rattle and then the sound of a strong wind. He prayed even more earnestly. The wind increased to a raging gale and the invisible hand of Him who is the *Lord and God of Storm* routed the French. Those who were not overcome by the storm returned to France.

GOD'S PROVIDENCE GUIDED THE PILGRIMS

Even after the Pilgrims arrived at Plymouth, you may recall that it looked very inhospitable. They had been heading for Virginia. Now they found themselves far to the north. They realized the weather would be too inclement for their settlement, so they decided to board the *Mayflower* again and sail farther south. They did not know that the east coast of America, as one historian says, "bristled with tomahawks and hostile Indians," and there was hardly one spot where they might have survived. One of the fiercest tribes dwelt near Plymouth, but because a plague had come across that portion of land several years before, almost all of them had died and they left nothing but the corn that enabled the Pilgrims to survive the first winter.

The Pilgrims tried to leave and were sailing south to warmer climes when *He who plants His footsteps in the sea* blew again, and the waves rose and fell, and the winds blew, and the *Mayflower* turned around and headed north and returned to Plymouth—the only place where they could have survived.

PROVIDENCE AND THE WAR OF INDEPENDENCE

Still, during the American War of Independence a Brooklyn woman almost made us all British. Washington and his whole army were trapped in Brooklyn Heights. The army surrounded him. The British fleet lay offshore. There was no escape. Night had come. The British general said, "We will wait for the morning. There is no place they can go, and we will destroy them then."

Washington decided to gather all the rowboats and little sloops he could and steal away under cover of night. His general said, "Sir, the frigates will be able to see us on the water. We will be blown to smithereens."

Washington said, "Do as I have told you." They began to load the boats. A Brooklyn woman, whose sympathies lay with Great Britain, saw what was happening, and she sent her servant to hurriedly visit the British lines and tell them what Washington was doing and stop the escape. The servant rushed to the opposing lines, and when he got there he told them, "Washington is filling his boats with his men. He is going to escape. You must stop him."

"Huh?"

"Washington."

They couldn't understand him. He said it again and again and they could not understand what he was saying. He had rushed right into the Hessian lines—the German mercenaries hired by the British to fight against Washington. They spoke no English, and the servant could not be understood, but they kept him there. In the morning they brought a translator. The servant told them what Washington was going to do, which by now he had already done. With the morning light they saw that his whole army had vanished! A fog had rolled in and covered the entire area just as they began to get into the boats. *He who plants His footsteps in the sea* had blown again.

Then, of course, there was the trouble at Trenton when Washington's artillery was stuck in the mud, and he couldn't move his army. He was trapped. The mud was so thick he couldn't get away. Night fell and again the British general said, "Washington is trapped. He cannot move. We will destroy him in the morning." And the *God of Storms* blew again. The wind changed and came down from the north, the temperature plummeted, the mud froze, and Washington easily rolled his cannons away on the frozen ground. When morning came, again he and his artillery had vanished!

You see, all we needed was a very clever general. Well, dear friends, if that were the case, let us look at what happened at Yorktown. Cornwallis was one of the greatest of the British generals, but now he was trapped at Yorktown. He had no place to go. The American forces had surrounded the fort. He knew that tomorrow it would all be over, but knowing the exploits of Washington, he decided to take a page right out of his book of tactics. So that night he had all of his British soldiers get into rowboats with whatever they had. He had gotten most of his army in the boats and off the shore, when *He who rules the waves* blew again and those waves rose up and swamped their boats so that they were flailing in the waves and trying desperately to get back to the shore.

The following morning, Cornwallis, carrying a white flag of surrender, walked between the twin lines of the American troops, along with his entire army, to the slow drumbeat of defeat. Religious liberty had been guaranteed and America was free!

Said George Washington, "The hand of Providence has been so conspicuous in all this [the course of war] that he must be worse than an infidel that lacks faith [who does not recognize and adore that invisible hand]."

GOD'S PROVIDENCE IN OUR LIVES

That same Providence works in every one of our lives as well. A familiar hymn says: "If thou but suffer God to guide thee." Another hymn says, "Lead on, O King Eternal." However, I do believe that many Christians think little about such guidance and providential leading. They get up in the morning and say, "Let's see what is on my agenda for today. What shall I do?" rather than saying, "O God, lead me, O Thou great Jehovah. What will You have me to do today?"

Ah, dear friend, the guidance of God is just as real in our individual lives as it is in the lives of nations. The Bible, in fact, says: *"For all who are led by the Spirit of God are sons* [children] *of God"* (Romans 8:14). Have you yielded yourself to the guidance and providential leading hand of God? His children have. His banner over us is love, and His plan for our lives is more glorious, more wonderful, more satisfying, more fulfilling than anything we might conceive ourselves. Dear friends, when you wake up tomorrow morning, and every morning, will you remember, and will you pray, and will you mean, "Guide me this day, O Thou Great Jehovah"? If so, you will be amazed what the years will unfold.

Remember. Remember Him so that you may not be found among those who have "forgotten Him days without number." Remember our God and Savior. Each day, knowing of our God's great providential watchful care over us, may we seek His providence in our own lives, and may we consider the invisible hand of *Him who plants His footsteps in the sea and rides upon the storm*, and who brought us to this land of freedom.

This is an edited version of the sermon "Lest We Forget," which Dr. D. James Kennedy delivered to his congregation at Coral Ridge Presbyterian Church on May 24, 1998.

Chapter 3

THE COST OF FREEDOM

*Therefore if the Son makes you free,
you shall be free indeed.*

— John 8:36

The world's finest news commentator, at least in my humble opinion, is Paul Harvey. He once told a story about a group of scientists who had decided that they were going to teach a chimpanzee how to write, and for fourteen years they labored indefatigably to that end. Finally the great day arrived when the chimp seemed to be actually forming letters into words—into an intelligible message.

The scientists rushed into the laboratory and watched breathlessly. At last the world's most pampered, best cared for, best fed, best housed, best trained chimpanzee in the history of mankind and the whole world was about to write the first message written by an animal. The excited scientists pressed forward to catch the history-making sentence. The chimp wrote, "LET ME OUT OF HERE!"

So too, countless millions of people living in totalitarian cages in Nazi Germany, and the Soviet Union, and all the communist countries around the world, including Cuba, our next door neighbor, have at great risk to life and limb said, "Let me out of here!" Many have died in their attempts to gain liberty and freedom. It is something that we easily take for granted. It is like the air we breathe and it is not until it is gone that we even think about it.

John Adams, our second president, made a declaration to future generations when he said, "Posterity: You will never know how much it has cost my generation to preserve [procure] your freedom. I hope you will make good use of it."

Have we? I am afraid that recent years would not demonstrate that we have. I thought it was interesting to read recently that the Second Congress of the United States passed a law stating that all U.S. coins would have on the reverse side an image of freedom, of liberty. These were rendered in many different forms. Instead of doing what monarchies have done, putting the faces of kings on their coins, they wanted the American people to be constantly aware of the precious gift of liberty. So every time they handled a coin, they were to be reminded of the preciousness of that wonderful gift and not take it for granted.

How have we done? Well, in the last few decades, the last of those coins disappeared. There is not one single current circulated coin with any image of liberty upon it. I am afraid, dear friends, that we are in danger and jeopardy of losing that which we have come to take for granted.

A LOCAL EXAMPLE

We have had a clear picture of that set before us here in South Florida during the last few months—the case of Elian Gonzales. His mother gave her life saying, "Let me out of here!" But what has happened?

One young lady recently said to me, "You do believe he ought to go back to Cuba to be with his father, don't you? You believe in family values. Isn't that right?"

I replied, "That is right that I believe in family values, and I believe that ordinarily a child ought to be with his parents. But all freedoms and privileges are limited. We have a freedom of speech, but you can't scream 'Fire' in a crowded theater, or you will suddenly find that you didn't have the freedom you thought you had. That is true in this case as well." Then I asked her, "If this boy's father were a child molester, would you want to send him back?"

"Of course not."

"If, indeed, he was abusive to his wife, would you want a child to grow up in that circumstance, in which case the child usually becomes an abuser too?"

"No, I wouldn't want that."

"If this were fifty years ago, would you want to send him back to Nazi Germany?"

"Of course not."

I said, "Well, the same thing is true here."

I recall hearing a debate a few weeks ago in which a very liberal congresswoman was talking about this situation and someone asked her the question, "Would you send him back to Hitler's Nazi Germany?"

She said, "That question is totally irrelevant."

If I had been there, I would have said, "No, it's not. It is a strange irony that American liberals seem quite able to see the evils of right-wing tyranny, but they seem to be totally blind to the evils of left-wing tyrannies. Millions of people have died trying to escape from communism, and you would send this boy back to that?" That is a strange irony, and it seems to say that American people do not treasure liberty like they once did.

COMMUNIST REEDUCATION

The other day we saw in the newspaper a photograph of little Elian wearing the uniform of the Communist Youth of Cuba. Isn't it wonderful—they brought a teacher up here to teach him. They didn't want to neglect his education. But what is he learning? I am sure he is learning what students learn in every school in every communist country that has ever existed. They are learning the wonders of atheism. They are learning the wonders of communism. It is the reeducation camp that has been seen in every communist country in the world. Should somebody wander from the party line, he will be reeducated one way or the other.

I can't help but think of George Orwell's *1984*, the book that caused millions of people around the world to actually hold their breath when 1984 arrived, as if suddenly we were going to find ourselves in the "land of Big Brother." (By the way, Orwell in his youth was a communist—very sympathetic as a British youth until he went to live in the Soviet Union. He came back absolutely appalled by what he had seen of the monstrous tyranny of communism, and he wrote *1984*.)

But it doesn't happen suddenly; it happens gradually. The hero in Orwell's book finally escaped from this total tyrannical land in which he lived, where Big Brother was watching him and controlling all of his speech and actions and everything about his life. He rebelled and he fled, but Big Brother caught up with him and placed him in one of their reeducation prisons and he was trained until finally he not only submitted, but the final words of the book are the most ominous of all: "Big Brother, I love you."

That is what can be done to a human mind, and I would not be surprised, that given enough time, should the court allow him the choice of going back to Cuba or remaining in America—and he has emphatically said, "I don't want to go to Cuba. I want to remain in America"—I would not be surprised if you hear him say, "Oh, I want to go to Cuba." Then we will all be treated to a photograph of him hugging "Big Brother" Fidel.[1]

THE BURNING FLAME OF LIBERTY

What has happened to that burning flame of liberty that so moved the Founders of this country? I am afraid the flame is burning very weakly in America today.

"Liberty." Abraham Lincoln said, "Our fathers brought

---

[1] One month after this sermon was preached, Elian returned to Cuba with his father. In a 2005 interview with *60 Minutes* Elian stated that he viewed Fidel Castro "not only as a friend, but as a father."

forth upon this continent a new nation, conceived in… [what?]… in *liberty*…!" Our Declaration of Independence says that next to life itself, the most important right we have is liberty. Many Bible scholars agree that the major theme of the entire Old and New Testaments is "liberty… freedom." Did you ever think about that?

Because of their sin, our first parents lost their lease on Paradise and in the bondage and tyranny of sin they were cast out. We then read how the people of God found themselves in slavery in Egypt for 430 years. Finally God sent a deliverer and they were released. But later we read how they rebelled against God and they sinned and everyone did what was right in his own eyes. We see in the book of Judges that over and over again the people sinned and they came into the prison house of some despot nation around them, one after another until finally God would send a deliverer and they would be set free. Then they sinned again, and again they lost their liberty and freedom. And this happened again and again and again and again….

When Nebuchadnezzar and his mighty hosts came from Babylon, they took them away with fish hooks in their lips and they served the Babylonians for 70 years.

The message is clear. Turn away from God and you end up prisoner either of your own sin or of some tyrant. So the whole Old Testament deals with that theme. Then along comes the Great Emancipator, Jesus Christ, to set men free, and to the Jews of His day He said, *"If the Son makes you free, you shall be free indeed"* (John 8:36).

What was the Jews' response? It is one of the most humorous and ironic statements to be found anywhere in the Bible, I think. They said, with a straight face, *"We are Abraham's descendants, and have never been in bondage to anyone. How can You say, 'You will be made free'?"* (John 8:33). I don't know why it doesn't say that Jesus laughed out loud—maybe because He pitied them. But they had been in bondage to the Egyptians and to the Babylonians and to everyone else that came down the pike for many centuries, and at that time they were in bondage to the Romans even as they spoke those silly words.

But Jesus was talking about the heart and source of bondage, which is sin. He said that if we commit sin, we are a bond slave, as the Greek text says, a *doulos* of sin. So it is sin that inevitably enslaves people—whether it be through alcohol or tobacco, cocaine or crack, sex or whatever—sin is always addictive, and it brings people into slavery.

THE REAL EMANCIPATION PROCLAMATION

Christ came ultimately to deliver us from the bondage, from the thrall of sin. Shackles are broken at Calvary. There on the cross, taking our sin and guilt upon Himself, Christ broke the chains of sin and set the prisoners free.

The Cost of Freedom

As one of our own said,

> Freed from guilt and free from shame,
> I'm free to serve and glorify His name.
> With joy in my heart and peace in my soul,
> Each new day to play out my role…
> As one who has been emancipated.

Do you know the Emancipation Proclamation, the *real* Emancipation Proclamation? Let me quote it for you. Don't ever forget it. *"Sin shall not have dominion over you"* (Romans 6:14). Only Christ could bring that to pass. Christ delivers us from the shackles of sin. He delivers us from its guilt. He delivers us from its claim. He delivers us from its power, and when we get to Heaven, He will deliver us entirely from its presence, and we will be utterly without sin. How glorious that is!

One great truth that I believe Americans have forgotten is the true source of the liberty that we have. It has come from only one place; it has come from God—it has come from Christ, who alone can make people free. Everywhere that people are free, it is because believers have been willing to put it on the line and stand up before the tyrant and say, "You shall go no farther." Once they have been made free in their souls, they have an irresistible urge for civil and political freedom. That is especially true wherever the pure Gospel of Jesus Christ—the Reformed

Gospel of Jesus Christ with its emphasis upon grace and the cross—wherever that has gone, it has been followed by civil and political liberty.

We take our liberty so much for granted, and yet very few nations in the world really enjoy it. Religious liberty? We think that is just a commonplace. My friend, I want you to remember that until the Constitution of the United States was signed, religious liberty had never existed in any nation on earth. The most the world had seen was in England where they had religious toleration, but that is all.

RELIGIOUS LIBERTY IN JEOPARDY

Now we are quickly throwing our religious liberty overboard and when religious liberty goes, other liberties follow. There are many in our country who have sunk so far below religious liberty that they don't even want religious toleration. There are many in this country today who won't even tolerate religion—most especially Christianity. I think, for example, of a federal judge, Jennifer Coffman, who wrote a twenty-two page order, which granted the ACLU's motion to get rid of a number of offensive documents that were in the courthouses and schoolhouses of Kentucky.

So what were these despicable, terrible documents that were un-American and could not be allowed? There was:

- Abraham Lincoln's statement that the Bible is the best gift that God has ever given to man,

- The Mayflower Compact, the birth certificate of America,

- President Ronald Reagan's proclamation of the Year of the Bible in 1983,

- The Ten Commandments,

- And from the Declaration of Independence: "We hold these truths to be self-evident, that all men are created equal, that they are endowed by their Creator with certain unalienable Rights, that among these are Life, Liberty and the pursuit of Happiness."

These could not be allowed, and so all of them were struck down. When did this happen? This month.

Also, at a Willis, Texas, middle school, sisters Amber and Angela were seen coming into school with Bibles in their arms. They were taken into the principal's office. The Bibles were taken away from them and thrown into the garbage, and one of the teachers told the girls, "We don't tolerate this garbage in school!"

At the same school, a teacher told a 13 year-old boy to remove a Ten Commandments book cover from a book and told the boy to put his Bible away; he could not have it at school. Yet, John Adams said it would be impossible to govern the world without God and the Ten Commandments.

Yes, my friends, religious liberty is in jeopardy in America today, in spite of the fact that the first president of our country, George Washington, said that religion and morality are the twin pillars upon which government rests. Washington also said, "Let not that man claim the title of patriot who labors to undermine those pillars." Yet today that is exactly what is happening. You cannot put up a crèche or a cross on public property (the ACLU has seen to that). But the National Endowment for the Arts, funded by your tax dollars, awarded a cash prize to a photograph of a crucifix immersed in a jar of the photographer's urine. Yes, that kind of cross or crucifix America allows, and you pay for it—but nothing else is allowed. How tragic.

THE ADVANCE OF GODLESSNESS IN EDUCATOIN

John Dewey, the father of modern progressive education, so lionized today, started the movement that divorced God from education. He was also one of the signers of the *Humanist Manifesto*, written in the 1930s and rewritten in 1973 which states:

> We believe…that traditional dogmatic or authoritarian religions that place revelation, God, ritual, or creed above human needs and experience do a disservice to the human species.

They add: "No deity will save us; we must save ourselves." And that has been the basis of all of the great advances of our modern public education!

Professor Jacques Barzun, an eminent educator and author, wrote in the *New York Review of Books*: "The once proud and efficient public school system of the United States ... has turned into a wasteland where violence and vice share the time with ignorance and idleness…." The result: These schools have turned out at least 40 million illiterates. It is not only unsafe for the children to go to school, but should they survive the drugs and the other things, they may very possibly be killed. Today it is not even safe for teachers.

These are the results of godlessness in our country. That statement in the *Humanist Manifesto* could just as easily have come out of the mouth of Hitler or Marx or their followers. I asked someone today, "What was communism all about? What were they trying to do? Was it something to do with economics?" He wasn't really sure, so I said, "Well, let me give it to you from the lips of

Karl Marx himself. When asked by a reporter what he was trying to do, he said that he was attempting to dethrone God and destroy capitalism. Notice the order of priority.

Yes, my friends, I think Americans have come to the place where they take their religious freedom far too much for granted. Yet today many people look upon religion as an evil, not even to be tolerated, but to be removed.

TWO REVOLUTIONS

Let me tell you the story of two revolutions—the French and the American. The American Revolution took place immediately prior to the French Revolution. The French were encouraged by our success and set out to do the same. But they approached it from an entirely different direction. Alexis de Tocqueville, the famous French philosopher and historian, came over here and described the difference. He said the American Revolution was built upon God and Christ and the Scriptures. The French Revolution was anti-God, anti-Christ, and anti-Scripture. The result: The American Revolution was a glorious success producing the freest nation the world had ever seen. The French Revolution was an unmitigated horror.

The French even did away with the Christian calendar, getting rid of Anno Domini, "in the year of our Lord." I mentioned that phrase once in a sermon years ago, and the young lady who was transcribing the tape of my sermon wrote "ono dominos ??" Neither she nor a young man I talked to after the first service had the faintest idea what Anno Domini means—in the year of our Lord. Today you may frequently see "CE," which does not mean "in the year of Christ," but rather the "Common Era"—another effort to try to get away from Christ.

The French tried that, and they named the year of their revolution "Year 1." But after putting a woman on the altar in Notre Dame as the Goddess of Wisdom, they revealed how little wisdom they had. With Robespierre and the Reign of Terror, the horror began. Twenty thousand heads rolled in the streets of Paris and blood covered the city. Not only did this lead to chaos, but as always is the case when you turn away from the freedom that God gives, you end up with tyranny. The Revolution later ushered in the reign of Napoleon.

My friends, freedom begins in the heart when Christ sets us free from sin. Shackles are broken at Calvary and there alone. When that freedom comes, it gives us a great desire for the civil and political freedoms that men need as well. Would that the flame freedom and liberty, which burned so brightly in the hearts of our Founders, again be fanned into a flame in America!

THE FLAME OF FREEDOM

Some years ago I said to a young lady, "You know, as

Patrick Henry said," and she replied, "Patrick who?"

I said, "Patrick Henry."

She asked, "Who's that?"

She was a product of our public schools. Patrick Henry's sentiments are so opposed to the "better Red than dead" sentiments that were popular a few years ago, and to the apathy toward liberty and freedom that now so typifies our nation that he has been removed from school textbooks. Neither his life nor his words are taught in many of the histories of America today, and that, indeed, is tragic. He was the great eloquent tongue of the Revolution and was six times elected the governor of Virginia. Patrick Henry literally ignited the spark that started the American Revolution, which procured our freedom, and yet millions in America today have never even heard of him.

On that memorable day in the House of Burgesses in Virginia, when the war had already begun around Boston and the "shot heard round the world" had been fired, Americans were dying in the streets, but most of America was not willing to get into the fight. They were crying, "We must have peace, peace. You will bring death among us if you opt for war. We are not strong enough. England is the mightiest nation with the greatest army and navy in all of the world. We cannot possibly take on such a foe."

Then Patrick Henry unfolded his long lanky frame and rose to his feet in the House of Burgesses. (I have stood in that very pew in the House of Burgesses where he gave that speech and I was filled with a certain sense of awe). He began to speak, we are told by eyewitnesses, very softly. All eyes were upon him.

> ... They tell us, sir, that we are weak—unable to cope with so formidable an adversary. But when shall we be stronger? Will it be the next week, or the next year? Will it be when we are totally disarmed, and when a British guard shall be stationed in every house? Shall we gather strength by irresolution and inaction? Shall we acquire the means of effectual resistance by lying supinely on our backs, and hugging the delusive phantom of Hope, until our enemies shall have bound us hand and foot?
>
> Sir, we are not weak, if we make a proper use of the means which the God of nature hath placed in our power. Three millions of people, armed in the holy cause of liberty, and in such a country as that which we possess, are invincible by any force which our enemy can send against us.

And though he began softly, by the time he had finished they said that it seemed that the walls and rafters rang with his words, and thunderbolts seemed to strike among the people—these people who were so fearful of engaging in the war for independence.

When he had completed this speech, the people were absolutely stunned. They had moved up in their seats. They were straining their necks. Their eyes were staring. They could not believe what they were hearing. Then finally, when he finished, there was silence ... total silence. Nobody moved. Nobody even breathed. After a long silence a cry rang out again and again. "To arms! To arms!" and the American Revolution began with a Christian man who was willing to put it on the line. A man in whose heart there blazed the flame of freedom. He concluded with these words:

> There is a just God who presides over the destinies of nations, and who will raise up friends to fight our battles for us. The battle, sir, is not to the strong alone, it is to the vigilant, the active, the brave. Besides, sir, we have no election. If we were base enough to desire it, it is too late to retire from the contest. There is no retreat but in submission and slavery. Our chains are forged, their clanking may be heard upon the plains of Boston. The war is inevitable—and let it come! I repeat it, sir, let it come!

> It is vain, sir, to extenuate the matter. Gentlemen, they cry "Peace, peace," but there is no peace. The

war has actually begun. The next gale that sweeps from the north will bring to our ears the crash of resounding arms. Our brethren are already in the field. Why stand we here idle? What is it that gentlemen wish or what would they have? Is life so dear or peace so sweet as to be purchased at the price of chains and slavery? Forbid, Almighty God! I know not what course others may take, but as for me, give me liberty or give me death!

And so our prayer is that our God may grant in the name of the Great Emancipator Jesus Christ that the glorious patrimony which our Founding Fathers have given to us, which has been sifting silently through our fingers, may be preserved and He would deliver us from our apathy. For if not, what kind of America will we leave to our children and grandchildren? May the flame of freedom burn brightly in this nation once again and may there be a great revival and returning to God that we may also return to the great principles of freedom upon which this nation was built.

This is an edited version of the sermon "The Cost of Freedom," which Dr. D. James Kennedy delivered to his congregation at Coral Ridge Presbyterian Church, on May 28, 2000.

Chapter 4

A NATION WORTH FIGHTING FOR

*Righteousness exalts a nation,
But sin is a reproach to any people.*

— Proverbs 14:34

A NATION WORTH FIGHTING FOR

Imagine that the year was 1939 and you were of draftable age. Your country was at war. You might very well be asking yourself the question, "Is this nation worth fighting for? Is it worth my dying for?" Easy question to answer? Oh. I forgot to mention that you live in Nazi Germany. The question just became a little harder to answer, I trust.

On this Veteran's Day we might ask ourselves the question, "Is this country worth fighting for ... or for that matter, any?" The Christian Church down through the centuries has always believed that there is a great difference between a *just* and an *unjust* war, and though there are several criteria, the principal one of them is that a just war is always and only a defensive war.

For example, there is no doubt, as the terrible pictures have been seen by virtually every single person in America, that this nation was suddenly, with no provocation, unexpectedly attacked from the air on September 11, 2001, and that two of our most magnificent buildings were totally destroyed, along with thousands of innocent civilian lives. This is basically no different than when the German Stuka bombers came roaring out of the skies over Poland raining destruction, and within weeks that nation was brought to its knees. Or consider the time the Japanese bombers dropped their bombs and destroyed most of the American fleet at Pearl Harbor, taking several thousand lives, both military and civilian.

We could say with confidence in each of these cases

that these were, and are, defensive wars, and therefore just. The ominous struggle in which we are now engaged is aggressive and unprovoked and something which cannot be justified in the minds of reasonable people. Therefore, it was necessary that we take the action we have taken to put an end to the death of who knows how many millions of people who could eventually die through this awful scourge of terrorism.

THE QUESTION OF OUR TIME

The question then arises: How much is this nation worth fighting for and giving for? The more precious anything is—the more valuable it is—the more a person would be willing to pay for it. Let's look and see what we have and how valuable it is.

If we go back 500 or so years to a time when the old world was growing old and older by the year, decay and despair were to be found everywhere. But unbeknownst to any, God had saved in between two great oceans the continent of America as the last great hope of mankind for the latter times. I have not heard the phrase "the last great hope of mankind" ever mentioned in reference to any other nation except this one.

Just look at the physical attributes of what has been given to us by God. Here, from "sea to shining sea," God placed this magnificent land, which is most certainly of enormous value and worth fighting for. From the snow-capped mountains to the vast prairies now golden with grain, from the countless rivers and thousands of lakes, which make it fertile and green, God has given to us this abundantly productive land, which is virtually capable of feeding the whole world.

From our marvelous hills to our canyons that are grand; grassy meadows and billions of trees; marvelous forests, but no jungles, all make this land the envy of the world. Compare it, for example, to the howling wastes of the dry and arid and desolate looking landscape in Afghanistan. You would wonder that anyone would be willing to give his life for such as that, but they are. Considering what we have been given, how much more should we be willing to do so?

GOD PREPARED A LAND AND A PEOPLE

Having reserved this land in the midst of the oceans, God at last prepared a people. Those valiant pioneers, the Pilgrims and the Puritans, came to establish the particular sort of land that God wanted it to be—a land where Jesus Christ was King and Sovereign. As our Founders said: "We have this day [on July 4, 1776] restored the Sovereign, to Whom be glory forever." God gave us those hearty men and women, the Pilgrims and Puritans, who were, above all, people of faith. They were people who loved God with heart and mind and strength and soul; people who loved His Word and read it daily and determined to teach it to their children to bring them up in the nurture and admonition of the Lord.

Yes, this was and is a very special land—built upon the foundations of the Christian faith. Other than those who have been so benighted by a secular school system or are so biased that they are unwilling to look at the truth, there can be no doubt that this nation was founded as a Christian nation.

In 1892, the United States Supreme Court, after investigating every document with anything in it pertaining to the foundation of America, declared unanimously that all of these documents bear abundant evidence that "This is a religious people…this is a Christian nation." Those who refuse to hear this proclamation merely express their ignorance or their hostility to Christ and His Church.

In 1830, the famous French statesman, historian, and philosopher, Alexis de Tocqueville, came over to this country to try to discover what the secret of America's greatness was. He traveled from one end of the country to the other, back and forth and up and down. He wrote his famous work, *Democracy in America*, in which he said,

> … There is no country in the whole world in which the Christian religion retains a greater influence over the souls of men than in America,

and there can be no greater proof of its [that of the Christian religion] utility, and of its conformity to human nature than that its influence is most powerfully felt over the most enlightened and free nation on earth.

What did the Christian religion do for this country? It made it the most enlightened and the freest country in the world, said one of the great philosophers and historians of the 19th century. How true and how obvious that is.

In 1802, John Adams conducted the first study of literacy in this country and found that only 0.4 of 1 percent of Americans could not read and write neatly. We now have 40 million Americans who are illiterate. You see, we did get rid of God from our schools. So, as one of the great humanist educators said, "It doesn't matter that Johnny can't read. At least we have divested from his mind all of that religious superstition he brought into the school with him." That "religious superstition," of course, is Christianity.

Indeed, we have moved far from being the most enlightened country in the world. We used to rank first over and over again in competitions with other advanced nations. Today, in test after test with the seventeen most developed nations in the world in math and science, our country repeatedly scores last or next to last.

No, we have been duped and deceived, and more and

more our religious freedoms have been and are being taken away. One writer has put it very well: The problems we are experiencing today get back to the waning of that Christian influence that made this country a wonder in the whole world. If that waning continues, who knows what the results might be. We were given everything imaginable and desirable in our land. As it has also been said, "America is great because America is good, and if America ever ceases to be good, America will cease to be great."

FACING A TEST

I think that right now we are facing a test: Will this huge problem, which could grow to sizes that few of us would even imagine, draw us back to God, or is this going to drive us farther away and harden our hearts? It is well to remember that the same sun that melts butter bakes bricks, and each of our hearts is like one or the other.

Dear friends, we have had so many incredible blessings, not only in the natural factors that have been built into this nation, but also in what our Founders gave us and what their children and grandchildren built upon it. It has been such a joy and delight for people to come and share in it. Think of the great things that God has produced through this nation:

A NATION WORTH FIGHTING FOR

- Wonderful statesmen: George Washington, Alexander Hamilton, James Madison, John Adams, and Abraham Lincoln, who have been held up as ideals before other nations around the world.

- Great inventors: Henry Ford, Thomas Edison, Alexander Graham Bell, the Wright brothers, and countless others who have blessed the world with their inventions.

- Think of the magnificent pictures: Betsy Ross sewing the first American flag—a flag which later was to fly over the surface of the moon because of America.

- Astronauts: Among the countless heroes produced in this land.

- Evangelists: Billy Graham, who just celebrated his 83rd birthday by preaching to an enormous crowd of people the glorious good tidings of the Gospel of Jesus Christ. Not only Billy Graham, but America has produced Billy Sunday, Dwight L. Moody, Charles Finney and many others who have faithfully proclaimed the Gospel of Christ.

- Missionaries: The Pilgrims said it was their hope that they would at least be a stepping-stone to taking the Gospel to all of the nations of the world. That hope and prayer has been fulfilled. America has sent out a stream of thousands upon thousands of missionaries and has reached actually every single nation on earth.

- Even in its enjoyments: Baseball—how many millions of people have enjoyed that discovery. Football, basketball and many other pastimes have indeed enriched and enlightened the lives of many people.

- Magnificent music that has come forth, and so many other things we have enjoyed.

In spite of all of these, silently, and unbeknownst to most, the cold clammy hand of unbelief has reached up and touched every facet of all of the good things we have enjoyed in this world. That, indeed, is the great tragedy, because unbelief inevitably leads to spiritual decay and moral turpitude and transgression.

"A CITY SET ON A HILL"

In the first seventy years of the history of Plymouth Plantation, there was one divorce. They were a godly people. This nation was once "a city set on a hill" and was known for the purity and godliness, piety and morality of its people. Now, every facet of this land has been tainted with unbelief, passing itself off as some kind of materialistic philosophy or another, some kind of secular humanism, some kind of skepticism or atheism. Inevitably, unbelief, like a blight on a tree, doesn't create, it destroys, and it brings with it deadly diseases—diseases that take not only the body, but the soul and destroy both.

We have seen that and more in this nation in the past fifty years. We have seen what has happened in our schools, once places of safety, once places of academic accomplishment. Now we find that many children are afraid to go to school. Teachers, in some cases, are taking early retirement and are being diagnosed with the same psychological ailment that some soldiers face in the foxholes. Now many students and teachers do not feel safe when they are in our schools. This, of course, is a sad commentary on what happens.

Yes, we have taken God out of schools. We have put police dogs and metal detectors and policemen in. Is that a good exchange? I am sure many in the ACLU, would say, "That's a marvelous exchange. We'll do it any time." And yet, the results have led to the dissolution of the family, to the introduction of well over thirty different sexually transmitted diseases, an AIDS epidemic, fornication and adultery, which are endemic in our land, as well as perversion, homosexuality, and all manner of other flagrant sexual sins.

One of the new program series on television, I think, is called something like "Sin Cities." Now they've come right out and said it blatantly, though certainly what we've seen in past decades has been little else but that. My friends, that is what causes some people to say, "Well, I don't know. Maybe the slate ought to be wiped clean and we ought to start over."

I don't think that is possible. I am not in the least bit pessimistic about the future, however, because at the same time these ills have been going on—belatedly indeed, but nevertheless in reality—the Church of Jesus Christ has been making a comeback. Christians are becoming active. They are active in the culture. They are running for public office. They are working in schools. They are in our libraries. They are in entertainment—a decade or so ago there was only one Christian producer in Hollywood. Now there are several dozen of them.

Furthermore, we see more Christians sharing the Gospel than ever before. We find that the number of people in this country who have actually come to a life-changing, saving experience with Jesus Christ is growing dramatically. For that, indeed, I praise God!

CALLED TO SERVE

Earlier in this service, we had those who have served in the armed forces stand. But I want to tell you that all of you here who are Christians are "in the service." Perhaps some of you have been AWOL so long, you don't know what AWOL means—that, of course, means "absent without official leave." Some of you have been AWOL from the service of Jesus Christ. But we are called in the Scriptures to be soldiers of Christ, to follow Christ, the Captain in the well-fought fight, to serve in His army.

At the end of each pew there is a square wooden block with a carving that has six different scenes from the two most common pictures or symbols of the Christian Church to be found in the Bible. And what are they? Three of them are pictures of a family; the Bible repeatedly tells us that we are the children of God, and He is our Father, and we are brothers and sisters in Christ.

The other three have to do with the other symbol—that we are in the army of Christ, that we are soldiers of Christ, that He is the Captain in the well-fought fight. We are told that we are to take the Sword of the Spirit, which is the Word of God. By the power of the Holy Spirit we are to put on the whole armor of God, and we are to fight the good fight of faith.

That kind of army, however, does not kill people. The only statistics it would have would not be of those who have been killed, but of those who were dead and are now made alive—who have found the joy of knowing Christ personally, of experiencing His love in their hearts. They have seen their lives and their homes and their families transformed by His grace.

What a wonderful army that is, dear friend, and all of us are called to be a part of it. If you are not, you can enlist today. When you receive Jesus Christ as your Savior and Lord, you receive Him as the Captain of your heart, the One whom you are going to follow. You are going to use the power of His Word, the Gospel of Christ, to quicken the dead, to change the hearts of those who are in love with evil.

God says, *"All those who hate me love death"* (Proverbs 8:36b), and that they do. They love abortion; they love infanticide; they love suicide; they love holocausts; they love destroying people because they hate God. If their hearts are changed, and their stony hearts are taken away and hearts of flesh that love their God are placed in them, they will love life, and they will do their best to see that others come to know that life as well.

Dear friend, you used to see big posters that said, "Uncle Sam Wants You," but God Almighty wants each and every one of you in His army, the army of Christ, the army of life—that forever army that is changing and will change the whole world. Are you a part of that army, or are you AWOL? The enlistment office is open. You are all welcome, and no one is 4F.

Therefore, in this struggle for life and death may we all join those who are seeking life, seeking to bring the dead to life eternal, seeking to make known the love and grace and forgiveness of the Savior of the world, our Lord Jesus Christ. And may God use each one of us in that effort as He brings change to this nation in the midst of the present turmoil. May our Lord draw to Him many people who have been indifferent for years and now have suddenly discovered that their lives have no guarantee for tomorrow.

∽

This is an edited version of the sermon "A Nation Worth fighting For," which Dr. Kennedy delivered to his congregation at Coral Ridge Presbyterian Church on November 11, 2001.

ABOUT THE AUTHOR

D. James Kennedy, Ph.D. (1930-2007). Because of his internationally syndicated television and radio broadcasts, Dr. Kennedy was the most-listened-to Presbyterian minister in history. For 48 years, he was the senior pastor of Coral Ridge Presbyterian Church in Fort Lauderdale, Florida, where Evangelism Explosion International was launched. Kennedy authored 70 books, including the bestsellers, *Evangelism Explosion*, *Why I Believe*, and (with Dr. Jerry Newcombe) *What If Jesus Had Never Been Born?* He founded Coral Ridge Ministries (now known as D. James Kennedy Ministries), Westminster Academy, and Knox Theological Seminary. In 2005, he was inducted into the National Religious Broadcasters' "Hall of Fame."

Timely Information and Encouragement!

DON'T MISS OUT...

Sign-up for the *IMPACT Magazine and Devotional*, published monthly by D. James Kennedy Ministries.

Enjoy informative articles with a biblical perspective on timely topics, find out about new resources the ministry is offering, and follow along daily during each month with devotional material to deepen your understanding of scripture and refresh your soul! All in a beautiful 8½" x 5½" digest format.

Visit **www.DJamesKennedy.org** to sign up for the new *IMPACT Magazine and Devotional* today!